Sunny's Mittens

Sunny's Mittens

By Robin Hansen

Illustrated by Lois Leonard Stock

Printed and bound in China
through Four Colour Imports Ltd.

4   5

DOWN EAST BOOKS
P.O. Box 679, Camden, ME 04843

To Hanne, Nikki, and Lois

Sunny's mittens had holes in the thumb and a hole in the finger-tips. It happened because there wasn't any new snow, just old snow and ice. Sunny and her brother Alden went sliding on the long hill by the golf course on the flying saucer, and Sunny steered by dragging first her left hand in the snow, then her right—until she felt ice biting her fingers and thumbs. By then, it was too late.

And they were the Fox and Geese mittens Nana had given her for Christmas. Billie Jo, at school, called them tic-tac-toe mittens because of the Xs and Os in the design, but Sunny knew there were geese on her mittens, and foxes, and fences to keep them apart.

Sunny was worried about showing her mittens to Nana, but Nana only laughed.

"Looks like you've gotten all the wear out of those there is to get," she said. "They were getting too small anyhow."

Nana went to her yarn chest and brought out a grocery bag full of mittens. "I'm knitting mittens this month for everybody. Show me which kind you like, and I'll make you a pair."

Sunny sat on the floor by the chest and spread out the patterns and the old mittens. "Patterns" were single mittens to show Nana how to make that kind of mitten—instead of reading written instructions, Nana used these as examples. Some of the patterns didn't have thumbs or cuffs and weren't real mittens at all.

There were Snowflake mittens that looked like a snowy night in the back porch light.

There was a Crow's Foot mitten that looked like a crow or a chicken had walked all over it. Nana had made a baby sweater for Corey with crow's feet all over and baby chicks on the shoulders.

There was a striped mitten with the stripes standing up like furrows in the garden. Mom had a pair like that in bright blue and a blue so dark it was almost black. That was Mom's mitten design. And Daddy liked the Checkerboard mittens, which looked like they were made out of puffy striped tubes instead of yarn.

There was the Fox and Geese mitten she had chosen last time, and—what was that?

A white mitten she had never seen before, as fluffy and soft as a cloud, with pink and blue embroidery on the cuff.

Sunny smiled. No one else had mittens like that, with great big stitches and a kind of furry look, and a blue and pink braid hanging off the side.

"I want this one," Sunny told Nana. "What kind of mitten is this?"

Nana smiled. "My Lovikka* mitten? I bought it at the flea market. It's named after the town it came from in Sweden." She took it from Sunny and slipped her hand into it, wiggling her fingers around inside. "I don't have to knit you this kind of mitten. You can knit them yourself."

* Pronounced "low-VEE-kah."

Sunny was so surprised she almost couldn't speak. "But I can't knit anything!" she cried.

"Of course you can," Nana told her. "Didn't you start making a muffler for your father? Didn't you start making a potholder for me?"

"Sure. But I never finished them. The muffler's under my bed. Mom took the knitting needles out of it to knit an afghan with."

"Well, Sunny-honey, then you can knit these. They're much easier than a muffler."

"But don't you knit mittens with four needles? I can't knit with *four* needles!"

Nana just laughed. "It's easy. The only difference is, you never have to turn and knit back the other way."

"But how do you keep it from falling into four pieces?"

Now Nana laughed again and went to get her coat. "Come on. We'll have to get some yarn. It's super thick yarn, called bulky. And you can use my needles. I think size 10½ will be good."

When they went to the store, they saw all kinds of bulky yarn.

"It has to be wool yarn," Nana said. "because we'll shrink the mittens in the dryer after they're knit. And it has to be like Lopi yarn, not spun very tightly, so we can brush it up fluffy."

The yarn store had different colors of bulky, loosely spun yarn. There were pink and blue and different shades of brown. Sunny thought pink mittens and blue mittens like that would look like wads of cotton candy on her hands. She chose white so her mittens would look like little clouds, just like the mitten in Nana's chest.

The yarn was fat and soft in her hands on the way home, and it had a warm wool smell. At home, she and Nana wound the fat yarn into a great big ball that she could pull from the center, so it wouldn't roll all over the floor as she worked from it.

Nana cast on 22 stitches on three needles, all with the same piece of yarn. No wonder they didn't fall apart, Sunny thought. It's all the same piece of yarn, dummy. She was glad she had figured that out for herself.

Then Nana began knitting, pulling the three needles around into a triangle and knitting into the first stitch again, instead of turning and knitting back across, the way Sunny had done for the muffler.

"You use the fourth needle to knit with," Nana explained, holding her work so Sunny could see it.

"What happens when it's all full?" Sunny asked.

"Then the needle you're knitting from is empty, and you use *that* to knit with." Nana had gotten to the end of the first needle, that quick, and was starting on the next one.

Sure, thought Sunny, feeling a little stupid. Knitting with four needles was a lot simpler than she had ever imagined. It looked so impressive when Nana sat there in in the evening, her knitting needles clicking like mad. But Nana was really only *knitting* with two. The other two needles were just holding stitches until she got to them. That was the secret. It occurred to Sunny that people would be impressed with her too if she could knit with four needles.

Now Nana had finished another needle, and she handed the triangle of knitting to Sunny. "You just keep going clockwise," she told her. "You never turn around and go back." She raised her eyebrows meaningfully. "Neither does the clock."

Nana had stuck the empty needle into the first first stitch on the next needle so that Sunny would know where to start. Sunny remembered the verse her mother had taught her to help her learn to knit:

> In through the front door,
> Once around the back,
> Peek through the window,
> And off jumps Jack.

The needle was already in through the front door. Sunny wrapped the yarn once around the back, pulled the tip of the needle through the stitch so the new stitch peeped through. "Peek through the window," she whispered. Then she slipped the old stitch off the left-hand needle: "and off jumps Jack."

She said the rhyme over and over as she did each stitch. When she had knitted all the stitches on one needle, she had an empty needle in her left hand and the triangle of knitting in her right hand. Nana had gone off to get her own knitting, and Sunny thought, "Clockwise. I'm at six o'clock. Next is seven o'clock." She took the empty needle in her right hand, stuck it into the first stitch on the next needle, and knit a stitch.

I'm doing it, she thought. I'm really knitting with four needles!

When Sunny had started the muffler for her father, she had knitted back and forth and the knitting had come out bumpy. But when she had gone around twice on the mitten, she saw it was making a smooth surface, like a real mitten or the outside of a sock.

"Why doesn't it come out bumpy like my muffler?" she asked.

Nana was knitting on a pair of Crow's Feet mittens while she watched Sunny knit. "Because you never turn it over and go back."

"How much do I have to knit?"

"Knit straight up until there are eight rounds. Just count the stitches going up. When there are eight, not counting the ones on your needles, give it to me, and I'll purl a round for you to make the little ridge at the edge of the cuff."

When Sunny got to eight rounds, she was still saying the verse to herself, but she was getting faster. Nana was cooking supper. Sunny brought her knitting out to the kitchen.

"I'm ready for the purl, Nana."

Nana was washing lettuce leaves in the sink. "I can't do it right now. My hands are wet and they'd stick to the yarn." She thought about it for a moment. "Tell you what, Sunny. Turn it inside out." Sunny turned the knitting inside out. "Now knit one round. You'll be going in the opposite direction, but it'll seem the same. Keep going clockwise, but you'll start by knitting into the stitch you just finished. When you get to the end of that round, turn it right-side out again and keep knitting. There will be a little hole where you started that row, but we can fix that later, when we put on the braid."

When Sunny had made the purl round the way Nana said, it was time for supper. After supper, it was time to go home. Sunny took the knitting home to show her parents and brother.

That night she slept with the knitting on the bookcase beside her bed. It was still dark the next morning when she woke up and thought: "Can I do it without Nana?" She sat up and took the knitting off the bookcase.

She whispered, "In through the front door, once around the back," and it all came back to her. She knitted until her father knocked on her door to wake her up—four more rounds. After school, she had soccer and homework to do instead, but the next morning she knitted four more rounds before breakfast.

Nana had said to stop after eight more rounds to "take off the thumb." Sunny didn't know how to put on a thumb, and she couldn't imagine why Nana would take it off before it was on.

When she came home from school, she saw why.

"I called Nana, and she came over to take off the thumb for you," her mother said. "I told her you couldn't wait."

Sunny gave her mother a hug and took a cookie. "Thanks, Mom."

Now there was a hole in the mitten, with four stitches on a piece of string across the bottom of the hole and four new stitches above the hole. Nana had knitted a round above the hole and pinned a note to the knitting.

It said: "End in sight! Knit 16 more rounds and try it on. If it's to the end of your fingers, get your Ma to bring you over. P.S.: Can you get your thumb through the hole?"

End in sight! She had only started a couple of days ago!

Sunny sat down in the kitchen and began knitting like mad. Once a stitch fell off between the needles, but she could see the hole the needle had slipped out of, and she put the stitch back on again. By suppertime, she had knitted all sixteen rounds and wasn't even saying the verse any more, just "once around the back" and "Jack."

Sunny showed her mother, then she and Alden ran down to Nana's house. Alden went to watch TV in the living room while Sunny and Nana finished the hand part of the mitten. They rounded off the end of the mitten by knitting stitches together at the end of each needle every other round, and then again every round, until only six stitches were left.

And then Sunny broke the yarn a few inches away from the mitten, threaded it on a yarn needle, and slipped it through the last six stitches. She pulled the yarn up snug, and there was a mitten without a thumb.

"Can I knit the other mitten now and do the thumbs at the end?"

Nana shook her head. "No, you can't. Thumbs go real quickly, but they are super boring. So do it now, or you'll wind up like me—with a big bag of patterns instead of a big bag of finished mittens. It'll take you about the last half of "Star Trek" to finish that thumb once I get it started for you.

At the thumb hole, Nana took the four stitches off the string and put them on a knitting needle. Next, she made a stitch out of one side of the hole, then knitted four stitches into the bottom of the stitches at the top of the hole, and made another stitch in the other side of the hole. "You don't need this many stitches, so I'm going to knit a couple together right away," Nana explained. When she was finished, she had nine stitches on three needles. She tucked the finger part of the mitten down inside so it was out of the way.

"Just knit about eight or nine rounds, until it's up over the top of your thumb," Nana said.

Nana was right. It took no time at all, just to the end of "Star Trek." The 7-Up commercial wasn't even over before Sunny was knitting stitches together around the tip of the thumb. She now had a whole mitten with woolly tails hanging off the ends of the fingers and thumb.

She ran into the living room to show Alden.

"So what?" Alden asked, like a dumb big brother. "One mitten. Two hands."

"But it's finished! It's a mitten! A real mitten!"

"Your other hand's going to get wicked cold," Alden said slowly. "Might even freeze off. Like an Arctic explorer's. You could knock your fingers off with a hammer."

It took Sunny the rest of week to finish the other mitten. Once both mittens were finished, Nana showed her how to work the woolly tails into the rest of the knitting and close up some little holes near the thumb.

They found some pink and blue yarn in Nana's yarn chest, threaded it through the mitten so it would cover the little hole at the purl round, and braided it with some of the fat white yarn. "Swedish people use these braids to tie their mittens together to hang them up, or to loop them over their belts when their hands get too warm outside," Nana said. "It's real handy. They don't need clothespins."

"Do you know how to do the embroidery, too?" Sunny asked. "I've never seen you embroider anything."

Nana squinched up her mouth and frowned at the pattern mitten. "I don't. But it looks like to me that we can figure it out. It looks like you do it by counting the stitches you knitted."

Monday night, Sunny could hardly sleep. She and Nana had stayed up way past Sunny's bedtime to felt the mittens (by washing them in hot and cold water) and dry them in the dryer and brush them up with a scrub brush and then embroider them. When Sunny went to bed, there was a pair of mittens like little white clouds on the bookcase beside her bed, with pink and blue embroidered zigzags on the cuffs and braids for hanging them up.

While she was waiting for the school bus the next morning, Sunny could feel how wonderfully warm her new mittens were. Fresh new snow was falling softly, and the snowflakes that fell on her mittens didn't melt until she breathed on them.

Billie Jo came to the bus stop and noticed her mittens right off.

"Awesome, Sunny! Did your grandmother make you some new mittens?"

"No," Sunny said. "I made them." She smiled happily. The mittens didn't just warm her hands. They made a happy, warm place inside her, too.

You Can Knit Mittens Like Sunny's

Design Your Own Mitten

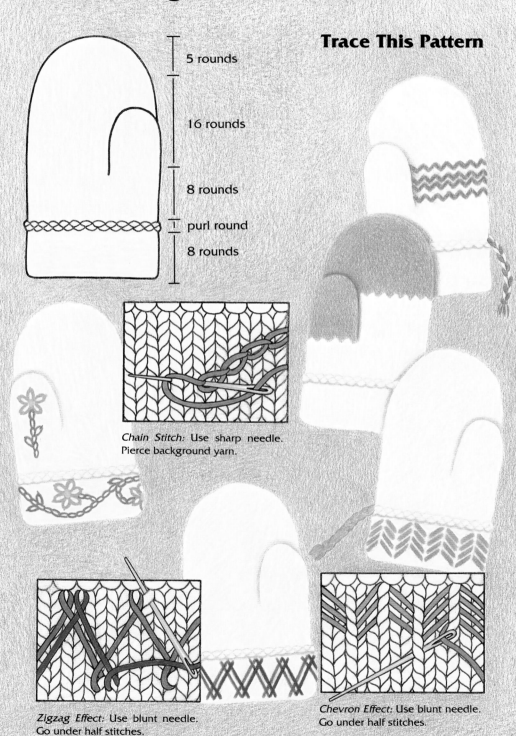

Trace This Pattern

5 rounds

16 rounds

8 rounds

1 purl round

8 rounds

Chain Stitch: Use sharp needle. Pierce background yarn.

Zigzag Effect: Use blunt needle. Go under half stitches.

Chevron Effect: Use blunt needle. Go under half stitches.

Recipe for Lovikka Mittens

YARN: One 4-ounce skein of Bartlettyarns Bulky (or another brand of big, fat, bulky yarn). Be sure it's real wool, so it will shrink. If your store doesn't carry it, you can order Bulky from Bartlettyarns, Harmony, ME 04942.

Or you can use a medium-weight yarn, doubled, but *don't wind it double.* Instead, pull the yarn from both the middle and the outside of the ball at the same time. Doubled yarn will be a little harder to handle than a single strand of bulky.

A 4-ounce skein will make about 2½ mittens for a child. The leftovers can be used for stripes on another pair of mittens or for a headband.

EQUIPMENT: 4 U.S. number 10½ or 11 needles, or the size needed to knit 2½ stitches per inch. Scissors. A yarn needle. A safety pin or a 6-inch piece of string.

TENSION: 2½ stitches per inch (See "Pay Attention to Tension," page 35).

SIZE: This mitten will fit a child about 8 to 11 years old. (For other sizes, see page 45.)

DIRECTIONS: Cast on 22 stitches on three needles: 7 on two and 8 on the third.

Knit 8 rounds for the cuff.

Purl one round. (Or turn and knit 1 round with the mitten inside-out, as described on page 38.)

Knit 8 more rounds, and then, on the side away from the beginning of the round, put 4 stitches for the thumb on a string or safety pin.

Cast on 4 stitches above the stitches you took off. (If you want stripes, just start knitting with another color. If the stripes are narrow, don't break the first yarn, just bring it up loosely when you want to use it again. When you do break the yarn, leave a 6-inch tail.)

Knit 16 more rounds. Try on the mitten. When it covers the end of the wearer's fingers, it's time to decrease.

Decreasing

First round: Knit two stitches together at the beginning and end of each needle. (22– 6=16 stitches left.)

Second round: Knit around normally without decreasing.

Third round: Knit two together at the beginning and end of each needle. (16 – 6=10 stitches left.)

Fourth round: Knit two together at the beginning and end of the needle that has four stitches. Knit two together at the beginning of the other two needles. (10 – 4=6 stitches left.)

Break the yarn, leaving a 6-inch tail. Thread the end through a yarn needle. Carefully slip the stitches, one at a time, off the knitting needles and slip the yarn needle through them. Draw the stitches together snugly.

CAUTION: Bulky yarn often is not tightly spun. When you sew with this yarn, be sure to first twist it a little in the direction of the yarn's spin to make it stronger, or it may pull apart.

1)

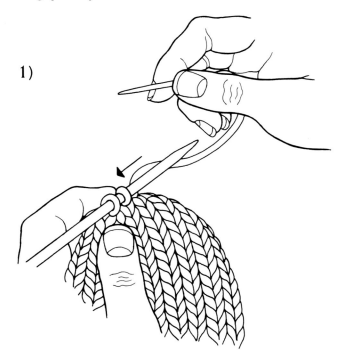

2)

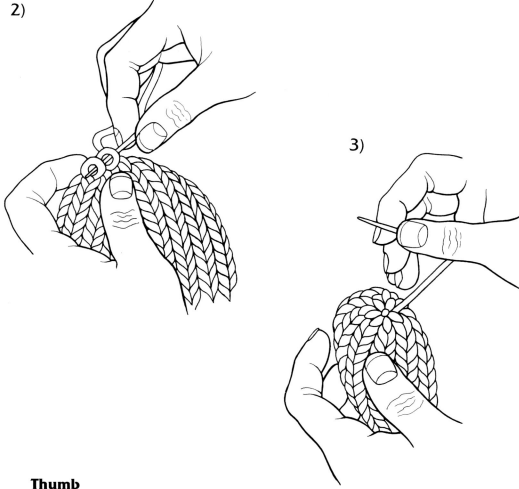

3)

Thumb

Pick up 10 stitches around the thumb—4 from the top, 4 from the string, 1 from each corner—dividing these 10 stitches evenly on 3 needles, with the 4 at the top on one needle.

In the next round, decrease one stitch by knitting together 2 of the stitches on the top needle ($10 - 1 = 9$ stitches left). Knit around for several rows, until the thumb of the mitten reaches just over the tip of the wearer's thumbnail. Decrease at the beginning of every needle for the next two rounds, then break the yarn. Pull up the remaining stitches on the tail, using a yarn needle. Work in the ends.

NOTE: At this point, the mittens will be slightly too long for the fingers and thumb, but they will shrink when you felt them (see page 40).

How to Wind Yarn So It Pulls from the Center of the Ball

If you pull the yarn from the inside of the ball, your ball of yarn won't roll all over the floor. To make this kind of ball, you will need a skein of yarn, someone to hold the skein while you wind, and a smooth stick at least 8 inches long, like the handle of a wooden spoon or a piece of broomstick.

1) Tie the end of the yarn to the stick.

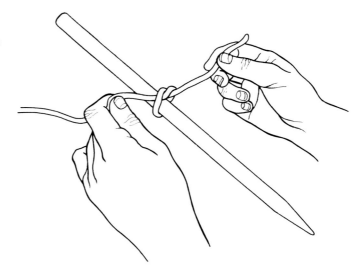

2) Wind a little to cover about an inch on the stick.

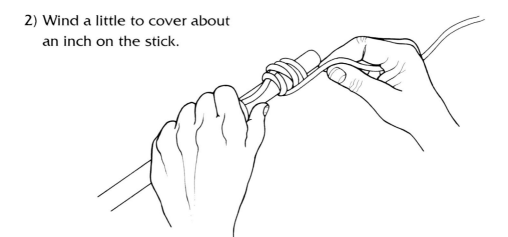

3) Begin winding diagonally, twisting the stick
   a little all the time to lay each turn of yarn
   next to the one before it.

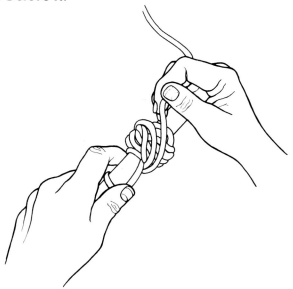

4) When all the yarn is wound up, wind the last ten feet
   or so around the ball and tuck in the end.

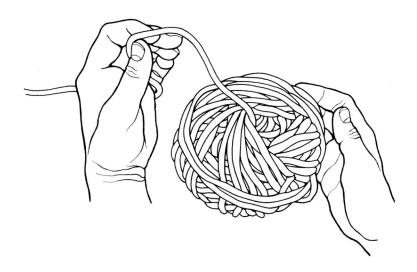

Learning to Knit

Hold your *left* needle on the palm side of your hand. Rest your *right* needle in the hollow between your thumb and index finger. You will control the tip of the right-hand needle with your right index finger and thumb.

Control your yarn with your right hand by pinching it in the crooks of your little and ring fingers. Or wrap it once around your little or ring finger.

This is a poem children have used for many years to help them learn to knit. Nana used it when she was little, too.

IN THROUGH THE FRONT DOOR,
Push the point of your right-hand needle through the front of the stitch, from the left side.

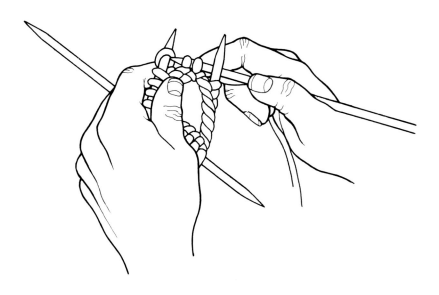

ONCE AROUND THE BACK

Wrap the yarn around the tip of the right-hand needle once and hold it pretty tight, while you . . .

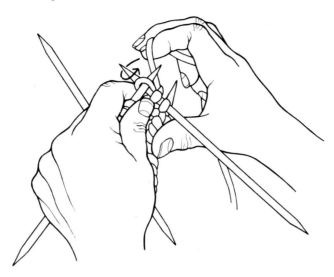

PEEK THROUGH THE WINDOW,

. . . slide the point of the needle back the way it came until it can peek through the hole with the new stitch still wrapped around it.

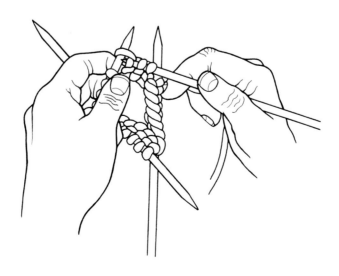

AND OFF JUMPS JACK.

Push the right-hand needle across the other needle so the new stitch will slide further down and not slip off. Then push the right-hand needle to the right so that the old stitch (Jack) hops off the left-hand needle.

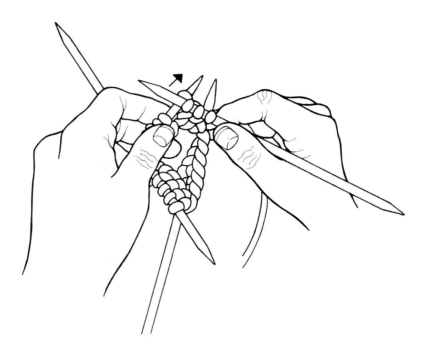

Pay Attention to Tension

Tension is also called "gauge." It means the number of stitches per inch. It's measured horizontally across the stitches, although some knitters like to know their tension both side-to-side and up and down. For these Lovikka mittens, the tension should be 2½ stitches per inch, measured across the stitches.

To find out how tightly you knit, start your mittens with number 10½ needles. Knit the first eight rounds and measure across two inches with a ruler. You should have 5 stitches (10 half stitches) in two inches. (One inch will be 2½ stitches, or 5 half stitches.)

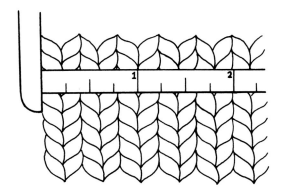

If you have knitted tighter, say 3 stitches per inch, *don't* rip anything out. Just change to the next size bigger by knitting the next round onto number 11 needles. It won't matter a lot if the wrist of your mitten is a little bit wider or narrower than the rest. If you bought new needles especially for this project, you can give the size 10½ needles back to the lady at the store in trade for the larger size.

If you've knitted looser, like 2 stitches per inch, change to a smaller needle. Try size 10, or even size 9.

Knitting on Four Needles

You are actually knitting on only two needles. The other two are just holding your knitting until you get to them.

When you have finished casting on to three needles, don't turn and knit back. Instead, bring the knitting around in a triangle, and start knitting with the first stitch that was cast on. This will hold the triangle together. Knit across the stitches on the first needle. At the end, you will have an empty needle. That's the one you will use to knit the first stitch of the next needle, and so forth.

Don't try to knit on fewer than four needles.

To keep your knitting even, always start working with the empty needle behind the needle you just filled (as shown in the drawings).

1)

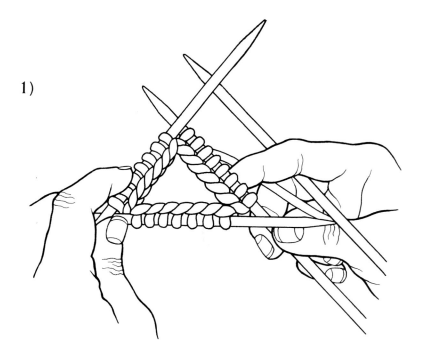

2)

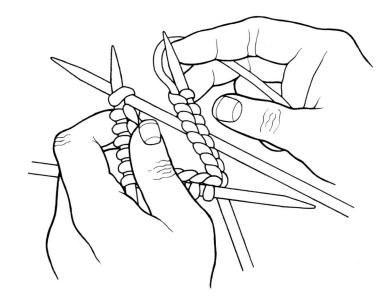

3)

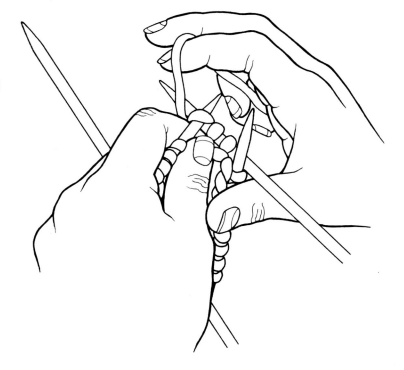

Knitting a Purl Round without Purling

Because you always keep working in one direction when you knit on four needles, your mittens will come out nice and smooth on the outside. The inside—the "purl" side of your knitting—has a bumpy texture.

Where the cuff of the mitten meets the hand part, though, you will make one round of bumpy purl stitches on the outside for decoration.

Purling is done the same way as knitting, but in reverse, and it takes practice. Nana showed Sunny an easy way to make that round of purl stitches without actually having to learn how to purl. Here is how it's done.

1) Before you start the purl round, turn your knitting inside out.

2) Knit into the stitch you just finished knitting. It will look funny, but just do it. Knit all the way around. You will still be going clockwise.

3) At the end of the round, turn the knitting right-side out again.

4) Knit into the stitch you just finished knitting, and keep going. When you get to the end of the round, there will be a hole. Pretend it isn't there and knit across it.

5) All the stitches you knitted while the mitten was inside out will show up as a round of bumps (purl stitches) on the outside of the knitting. On the inside of the mitten, they look like ordinary knit stitches.

Decreasing (Narrowing)

To decrease at the end of the hand and the thumb, knit two stitches together at the ends of the needles. This is just like knitting one stitch, except you go over one more stitch and push the needle through two stitches at the same time. It's a little harder than knitting one stitch at a time.

Finishing Your Mitten
And Working in the Ends

To finish your mitten, you must work the tails into the fabric, darning across any small holes at the thumb, and especially across the tips of the thumb and the mitten.

BE CAREFUL: Bulky yarn often is not spun tightly. Whenever you sew or darn with this yarn, be sure to twist it a little tighter in the direction of the yarn's spin to make it stronger or it may fall apart when you pull on it.

At the tip of the mitten, thread the tail onto the yarn needle and give it a couple of twists. You have already put all the remaining stitches on the tail, but now you should lock the tip of the mitten tight by pulling the tail through the first 2 or 3 stitches again, then pull the yarn through to the inside of the mitten. Do the same at the tip of the thumb. Pull any other tails through to the inside of the mitten and turn it inside out.

Still using the yarn needle, weave the tails at the tip of the mitten and the tip of the thumb into the knit with a running stitch, working toward the cuff, going under the bumps of the purl stitches and skipping every other bump. Do this for about 1½ to 2 inches, then cut the yarn close to the mitten and give the mitten a pull to hide the end of the tail.

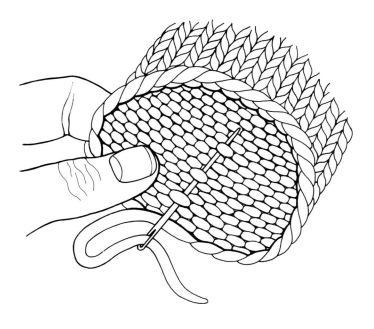

Hide the little holes at the sides of the thumb by stitching the tail across them a couple of times on the inside of the mitten, then weave in the end.

At the bottom edge is a long tail. Weave it in too.

There is a little hole where you made the round of purl stitches. This is where you'll put your braid. Take another piece of the bulky yarn about 12 inches long, thread it on the yarn needle and pull it through the mitten right across the hole so it hangs down 6 inches on each side. You can close the gap by pulling the sides of the hole together on the new piece of yarn. Thread 2 more 12-inch pieces of yarn over the hole the same way. You can make the braid all one color or a mix of 2 or 3 colors. Braid the strands together until the braid is about 4 inches long. Tie the end of the braid with a little piece of thin yarn.

When your mitten is finished, there won't be any tails hanging inside or outside, just the big decorative braid that you made on purpose.

Felting Your Mitten
And Brushing Up the Fur

Felting makes the little fibers in the wool mat together, the way they do after you make icy snowballs and then dry your mittens on the radiator. It also makes the mittens shorter, a tiny bit narrower, and much warmer. Wash and felt the mittens until they fit, but make sure they don't get too small.

You will need a basin of very warm (but *not* scalding hot) water and a basin of very cold water and some real soap—like Murphy's Oil Soap or a cake of Ivory—not detergent.

Soap up the hot water and put the mittens in. Scrub them between your hands with even more soap. This helps the fibers mat together. Do this for about five minutes for each mitten.

Rinse the mittens in icy cold water.

Soap them up once more and scrub them in the hot water again for about five minutes. (If the water has cooled off, add more very warm water to the basin.) Rinse them in a fresh basin of cold water.

To make the mittens very soft, put a tablespoon of ammonia into the second rinse, but then rinse them again afterward with plain water. Squeeze them out but don't twist them.

Brush the mittens with a scrub brush until they look a little hairy. *Don't brush the cuff band.* You need to be able to see the stitches on the cuff to embroider them.

Roll up the wet mittens in a towel and press on the towel with all your weight until you feel wetness coming through. They will still be damp, so put them in the clothes dryer or on the radiator until they are completely dry. (It's better if there are a few other things in the dryer at the same time to keep your mittens moving. Dry them at regular, not low, heat.)

When they are dry, brush them again, all except the cuffs, starting at the wrist and going toward the fingertips.

Decorating Your Mittens

If you've made colored mittens, or mittens with stripes, or mittens with the thumb and the tip of the mitten a different color from the rest, they don't really need any more decoration.

But if you have made plain mittens like Sunny's and want to add a little embroidery, the knitters of Lovikka, Sweden, have the world's easiest embroidery for you.

You will need the yarn needle, some different colored pieces of yarn, and a pair of scissors.

Remember to work the ends into the inside of the mitten. No knots please. If you are embroidering chain stitch, stick the needle right through the knitted stitches. This holds the embroidery in place. If you're counting stitches, put the needle between and under the knitted stitches. See the illustration on page 26 for embroidery instructions and examples.

This Is What Nana Did.
You Can Do It Too.

Casting On

If you have a knitter to help you, get her to cast on for you. That's the fastest and easiest way to get started. If you don't have someone to help, here is a very simple way to cast on. There are prettier ones, but this one works fine.

If you are a Scout or know how to sail, you may recognize this as a half-hitch. Casting on this way is just a long series of half-hitches.

1)

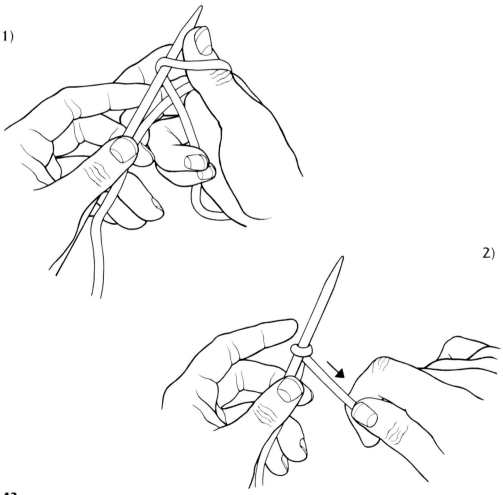

2)

Taking off for the Thumb

The thumb hole goes on the side away from the beginning of the round. It is four stitches wide. Use the first 4 stitches on the second needle for one mitten, and the last 4 for the other mitten.

When you are ready to make the hole, slip four stitches off your left-hand needle before knitting them. Use a yarn needle or a crochet hook to put a piece of string through the stitches to keep them from ravelling, or put them on a safety pin.

Cast on four stitches above the hole the same way as you cast on at the cuff. Better yet, get someone to do it for you. These new stitches will go onto the right-hand needle. You will still have a total of 22 stitches.

Keep knitting around. When you have knitted the 4 new stitches the first time, you may find that there is a loose place right at the end of them. Knit right past it. Don't worry about it.

Knitting the Thumb

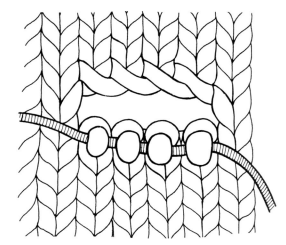

Thumb hole

Pick up 10 stitches around the thumb: Slide a knitting needle into two of the four stitches on the string or safety pin. Slide another needle into the other two and remove the string or pin.

Hold the mitten so the top is away from you. On the top of the thumb hole, use a third needle to pick up the left sides of four stitches right along the edge of the hole.

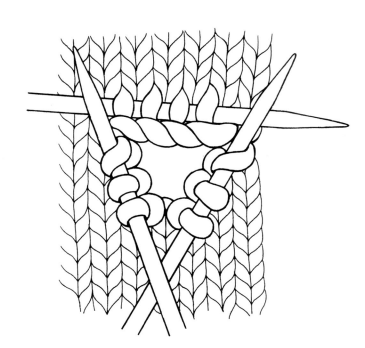

10 stitches picked up around hole

You will have to make an extra stitch on each end of the hole to fill the gaps between the two needles at the bottom and the needle at the top. Using the needles from the bottom, pick up the side of the stitch at each corner. Go in from the outside on the right-hand side of the hole. On the left, poke the needle through from inside the thumb hole. If you push the needle through the *back* loop of that stitch the first time you knit it, you will twist the stitch, and there will be less of a hole to patch up later.

You have 4 (top) + 3 (right) + 3 (left) = 10 stitches, but you only need 9 stitches. Begin knitting around with the top needle and knit 2 together on the top needle the second time around. Knit 8 rounds and slip the mitten on. If your needles are just above the tip of your thumb, it's time to decrease. Knit two together at the beginning of every needle until you have only 3 stitches left. Break the yarn, leaving a 6-inch tail. Thread the tail onto a yarn needle and give it a couple of twists to make it stronger. Carefully slide the stitches, one at a time, off the knitting needles and slip the yarn needle through them. Pull the yarn carefully until the last 3 stitches are pulled tightly together.

Getting the Right Size

These mittens will fit you, after they've been felted, if you have an average-size hand for an 8 to 11 year old. If your hand is much narrower or wider than your friends', add 2 stitches (24) or subtract 2 (20) when you cast on.

If you are knitting for a toddler, cast on 18 stitches and reduce the distance between the purl round at the top of the cuff and the round where you take off for the thumb to 6 rounds.

If you are knitting for a grown-up, cast on 24 stitches and increase the distance between the purl round and the thumb hole to 10 rounds. Everything else should work.

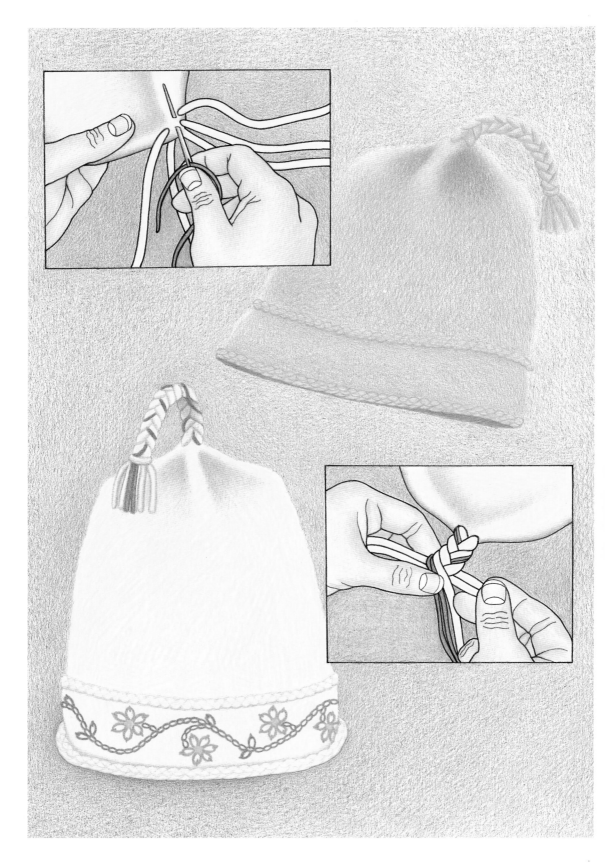

A Cap to Go with Your Mittens

There's nothing at all difficult about making a cap to go with your mittens, since caps don't have thumbs. Sunny made a cap in four days. She could have finished it more quickly, but she got a little tired of knitting around and around with no interesting things happening.

YARN: One 4-ounce skein of Bartlettyarns Bulky, or whatever yarn you used for the mittens.

EQUIPMENT: 4 U.S. number 10½ or 11 needles, or the size you need to knit 2½ stitches per inch. Scissors. A yarn needle. A ruler or other 6-inch measure.

TENSION: 2½ stitches per inch (see "Pay Attention to Tension," page 35).

SIZE: This cap will be 20 inches around, which fits most fourth-graders' heads. If your head is small, take off 2 or 3 stitches from the total of 50; if you have a large head, add 2 or 3 stitches.

DIRECTIONS

Cast on 50 stitches on 3 needles, 17 stitches each on 2 needles, and 16 on the third.

Knit 9 rounds for the cuff.

Purl one round.

Knit 22 more rounds.

Decrease

First round: Knit 2 stitches together at the beginning and end of each needle.

Second round: Knit around normally without decreasing.

Then knit 2 together at both ends of every needle every round until only 2 stitches are left on each needle.

Break the yarn with a 10-inch tail. Thread the tail on a yarn needle and draw up the remaining 6 stitches on the tail.

CAUTION: Bulky yarn often is not tightly spun. When you sew with this yarn, be sure to twist it a little in the direction of the yarn's spin to make it stronger, or it may pull apart.

Braid

(The illustration on page 46 shows how to make the braid.) Break 2 strands of bulky yarn about 12 inches long. Use the yarn needle to pull them halfway through at the tip of the cap. Break off a 12-inch strand of colored yarn in one or more of the colors you used for the embroidery on the mittens. Pull it halfway through next to the other strands. Divide the yarns in 3 groups, putting the colored yarn with the single strand left over from the knitting. Braid them together until the braid is about 4 inches long, then tie the braid with the colored yarn. Trim the end nicely with scissors and work any tails back in to the fabric.

Decorate your cap to match your mittens. You can also brush it some, to make it fluffy, but *don't* felt it.